iMac 2020 user guide

AF414970

BY

Piers N.Lowe

Copyright © 2021

Piers N.Lowe

All rights reserved. No part of this book shall be reproduced, stored in a retrieval system, or transmitted by any means, electronic, mechanical, photocopying, recording, or otherwise, without written permission from the publisher. Although every precaution has been taken in the preparation of this book, the publisher and author assume no responsibility for errors or omissions. Nor is any liability assumed for damages resulting from the use of the information contained herein.

DISCLAIMER:

The information contained in this book is for educational purposes only. All efforts have been executed to present accurate, reliable, and up to date information. No warranties of any kind are implied. The contents from this book are from various sources. Please consult a licensed professional before attempting any techniques contained herein.

By reading this document, the reader agrees that under no circumstances is the author responsible for any losses, direct or indirect, which are incurred as a result of the information contained in this book including errors, omissions, and inaccuracy.

Table of Contents

INTRODUCTION

The iMac is a series of Mac desktops designed by Apple as a cheaper form of their computer. It was designed to suite people who are new to using a Pc and other old Mac users. The iMac fits beginners and pro users, allowing them adapt to both normal and heavy usage. If you are comfortable with buying a full computer set which includes the mouse and keyboards, or you simply want to improve your work productivity, then the iMac is for you.

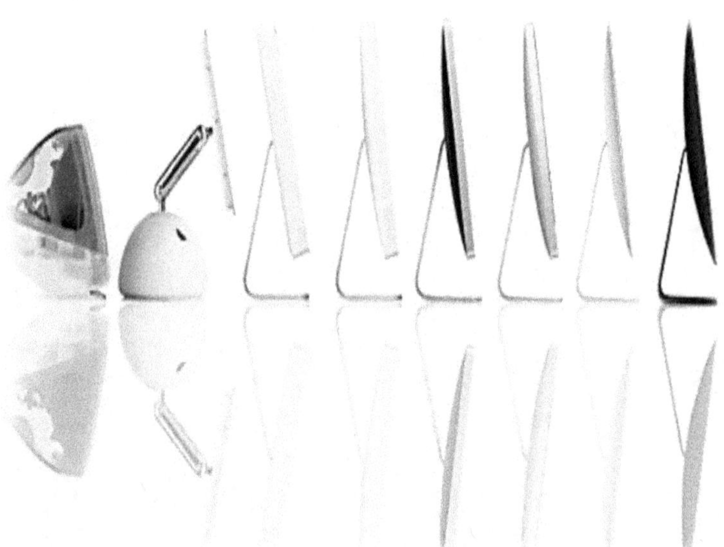

On the 4th of August 2020, Apple updated the 27-inch iMac to incorporate the 10th gen Intel processor, adding more RAM, more SSD memory and an enhancement in the speed of the AND graphics processor, as well as True Tone.

The update to the 27-inch iMac only refreshed the display and the interior of the iMac, while the body of the iMac received no upgrade.

Embedded in the iMac 2020 is Intel's 10th-gen chip which has around 10 cores and a Turbo Boost speed that can reach 65 to 5.0GHz to produce a faster CPU performance.

Also added to the iMac 2020 is Radeon Pro 5000 graphics which has a speed that is 50 percent faster than that of the previous generation.

To enhance security, the iMac 2020 is equipped with a T2 Chip designed by Apple which improves data encryption as well as software loading validation Security and more.

With the iMac 2020 offering up to 128GB of fast 2666MHz RAM, the iMac is two times faster than the previous generation. The iMac 2020 also has support for 1080p FaceTime HD camera. According to Apple, the iMac 2020 has a balanced high-fidelity variable EQ speaker, improved bass, and a studio-quality microphone.

Design

The design of the iMac 2020 remains the same with a 5mm, razor-thin screen, an aluminum rack, an aluminum frame and a sleek body. The iMac 2020 has a single connector at the back as well as a port to connect accessories. The iMac 2020 is around 20.3 inches in height, has a width of 25.6 inches, and has a depth of 8 with a weight of around 19.7 pounds. The iMac models with inbuilt Mount Adapter to mount iMac on walls are sold separately.

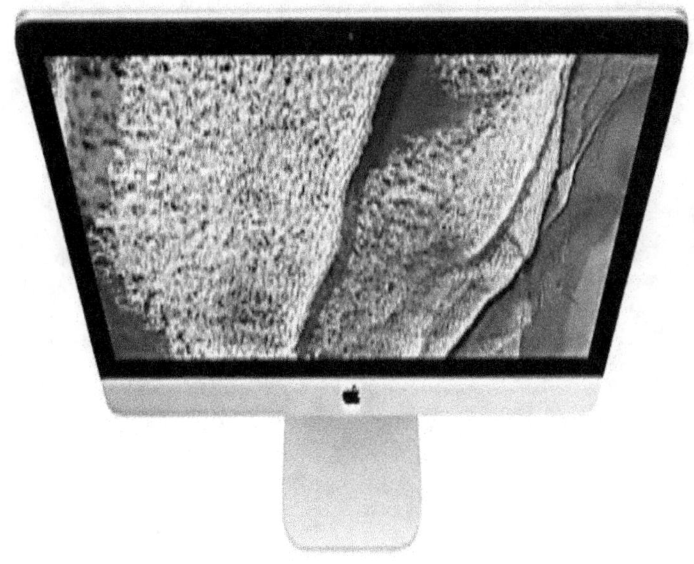

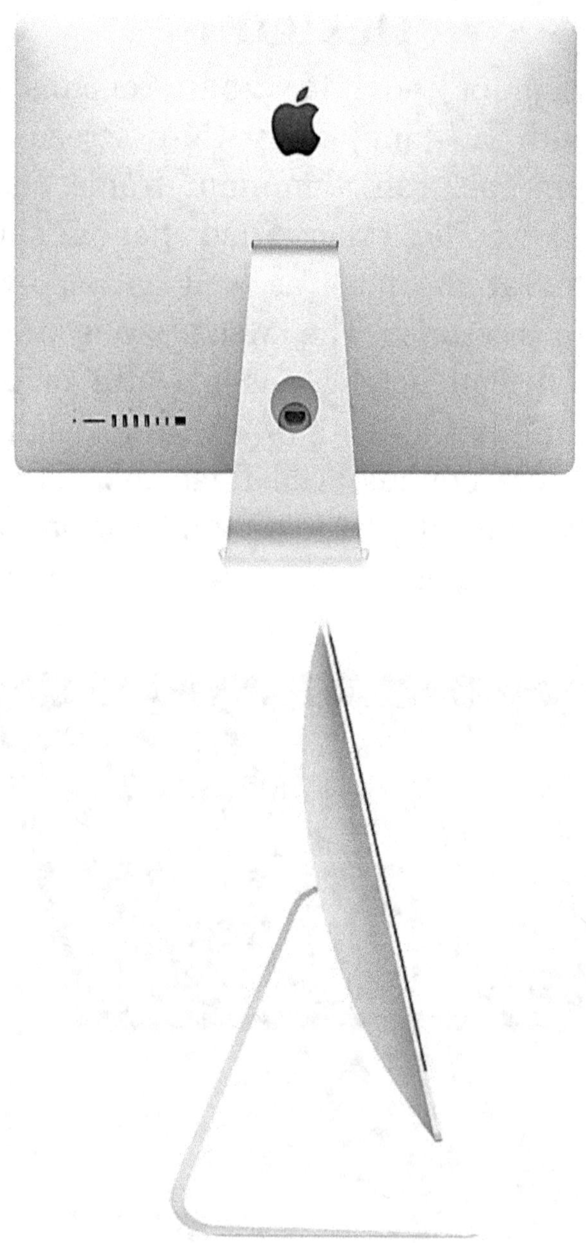

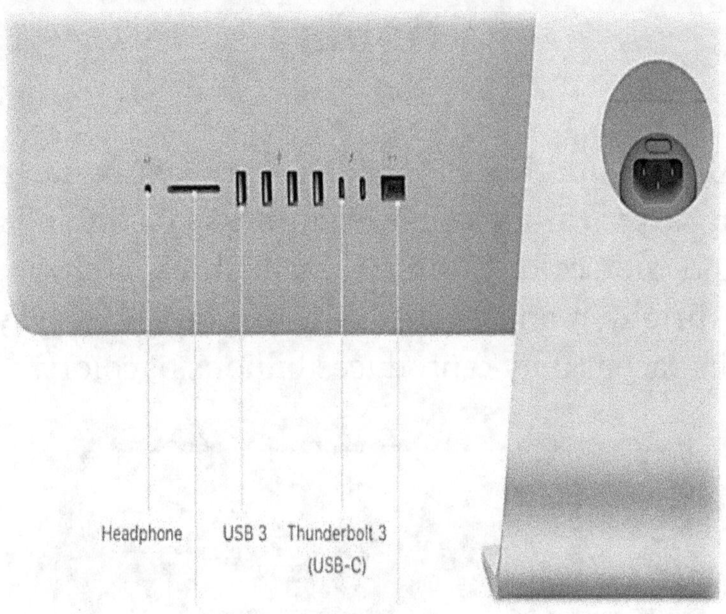

Headphone
USB 3
Thunderbolt 3
(USB-C)

Display

All 4K and 5K iMac models were last updated in 2017, with 500-bit brightness, 10-bit split, and wide color gamut. These features allow for a brighter and more vivid display, a display that accurately reproduces billions of colors.

The iMac 2020 has a resolution of 5120 to 2880, and it also has support for True Tone.

This is the first time True Tone has been added to an iMac display. The intensity of the screen matches the room light, which reduces visibility and reduces strain to the eyes.

27-inch iMac

Updated for 2020, the 27-inch iMac has a 5T display, support for 256GB or 512GB True Tone SSD, and a standard storage option that can be upgraded to 8TB.Supports 10th Gen Intel chips, Radeon Pro graphics, and up to 128GB at 2666MHz DDR4 RAM which is twice the amount recommended on previous models.

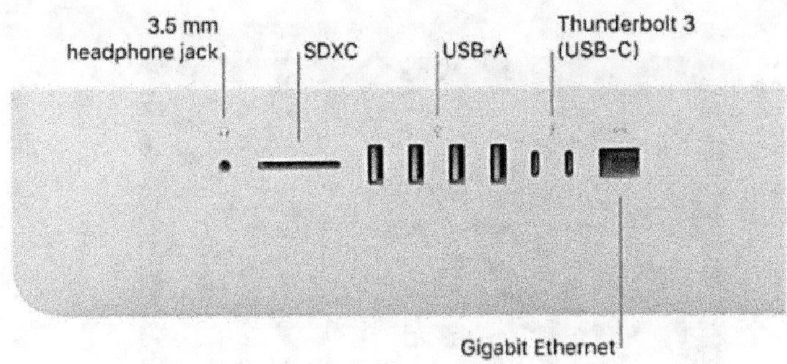

3.5 mm
headphone jack
SDXC
USB-A
Thunderbolt 3
(USB-C)
Gigabit Ethernet

Power button
AC power port

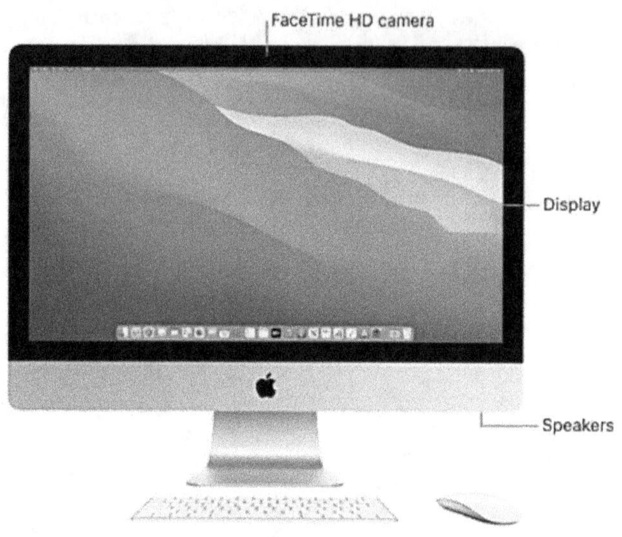

CPU and GPU 27

The iMac 2020 is powered by Intel's 10th-generation 6-core, 8-core, and 10-core processors, which offers speed improvements.

The 27-inch iMac has a 6-core 10th-gen Intel Core i5 processor at 3.1GHz, while the mid-range model has a 6-core 3.3GHz 10th-generation processor.

Premium Intel Core i5 processors have an 8-core 8th-core Intel Core i7 processor at 3.8GHz.Mid-range and high-end models can be upgraded with a 10-core Intel Core i9 processor at 3.6GHz, and 8- and 10-core chip options have Turbo Boost up to 5.0GHz

T2 chip

The iMac 2020 has the T2 chip which is responsible for encrypting data for everything stored on the SSD and helping you keep the software free from malware.

The T2 chip also provides an improved booting process.

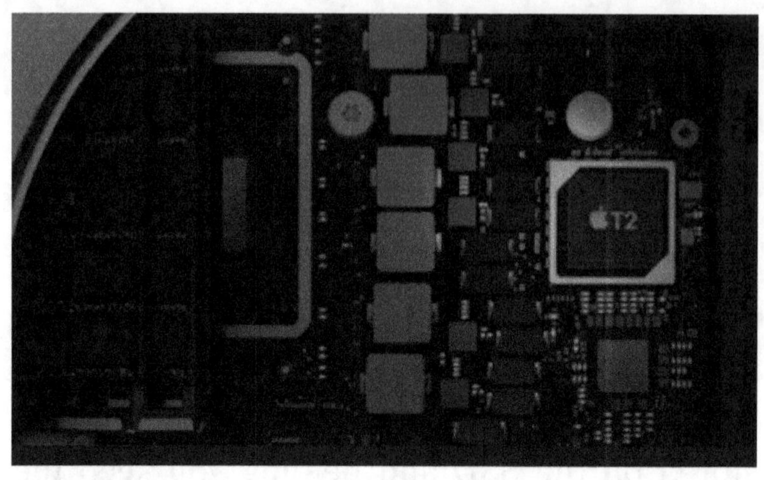

Camera, speaker, microphone

All iMacs have a FaceTime HD camera on the front. The iMac 2020 has a 1080p camera.

The 27-inch iMac's video signal processor offers travel photography, exposure control, and facial recognition.

All iMacs have built-in stereo speakers and microphones, but Apple is rolling out a 2020 upgrade to the 27-inch iMac.

Apple says the 27-inch iMac's T2 chip works with the speakers to enable variability to improve the balance, providing a tighter, deeper bass. There are numerous studio quality mics that help users get high quality sound.

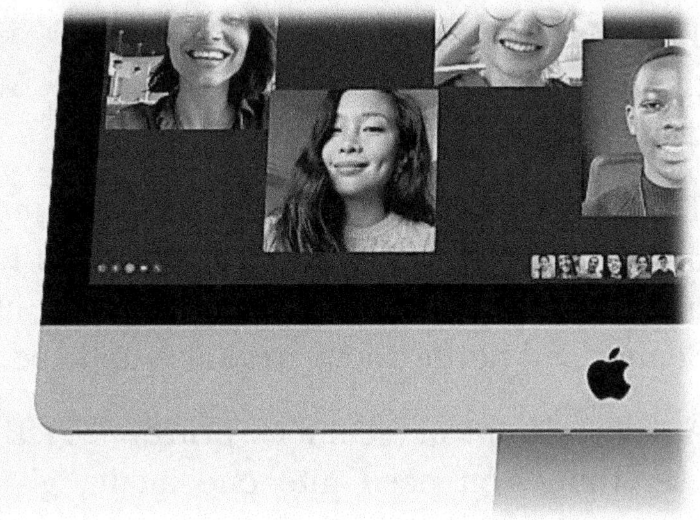

Connection

The iMac 2020 has support for Bluetooth 5.0 technology, while the 21.5-inch iMac supports Bluetooth 4.2

Features

The iMac 2020 has many new features with the macOS Big Sur which gives the Mac desktop a new appearance.

There is an updated icon menu bar with more menus, a full-height sidebar and built-in tool buttons which make the app easy to use. Sounds and notifications were also updated.

A new Control Center brings together everything you need into one menu, giving you quick access to your most-used controls and settings.

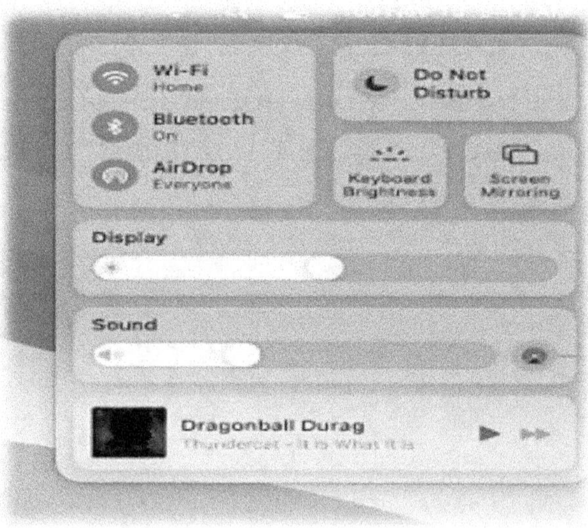

Safari has been updated to give faster search results. Users can now find and customize start pages, also having access to many extensions from the App store.

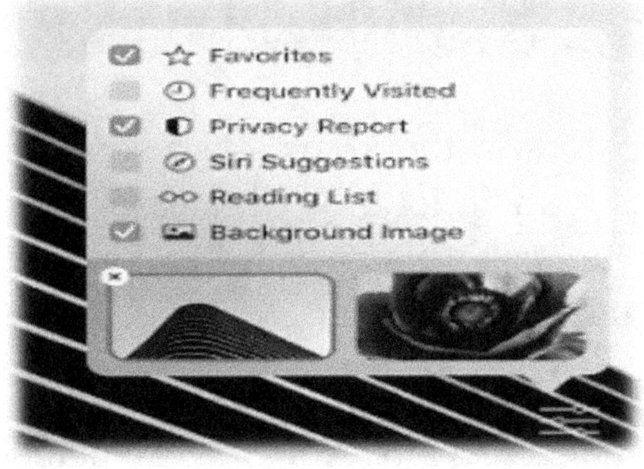

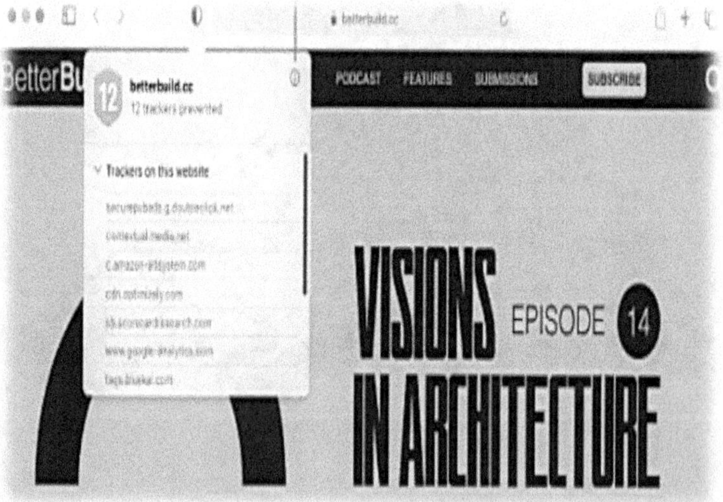

With new guides in the Maps app, users can find places in their locality with ease. This allows you to make plans on where to eat, shop or even travel.

Maps also have integrated Interactive 3D tour of the selected city streets. Now you can plan a bike route showing altitude and obstructions or your own route.

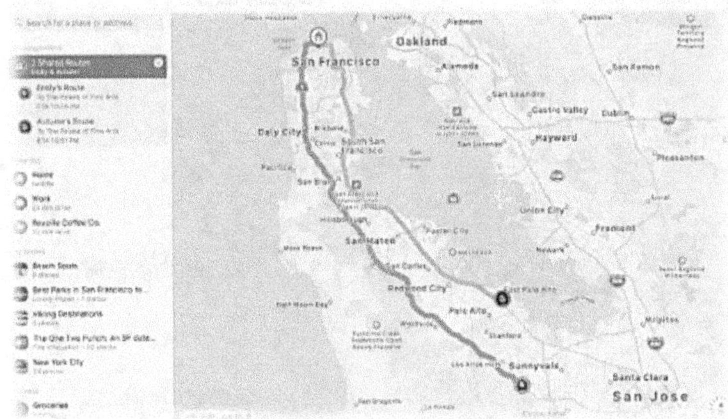

With new messaging effects, you can customize your messages. You can also add Memoji stickers to your messages that suit your mood and personality, and create new stickers using the Memoji editor on your Mac.

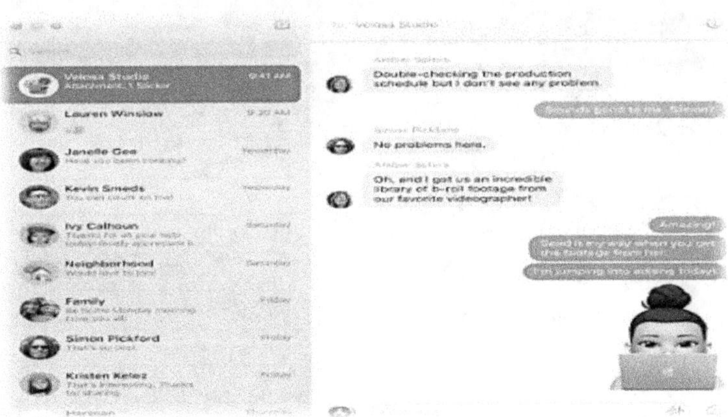

Tapbacks and new activity
appear over a group picture.

Pin favorites to the top.

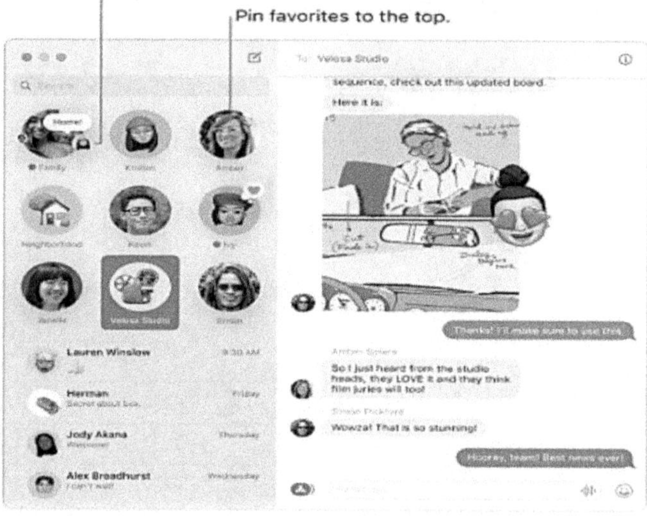

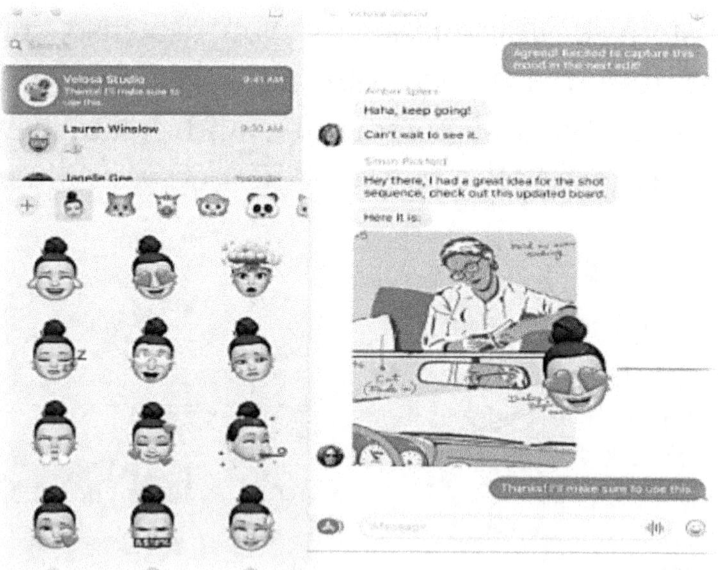

Unboxing

In the box, you have a Magic Keyboard and a Magic Mouse

To start using the Magic Keyboard and Magic Mouse 2, place the power button on each device on the power button

The magic keyboard which is also rechargeable connects automatically to your iMac when you want to use it.

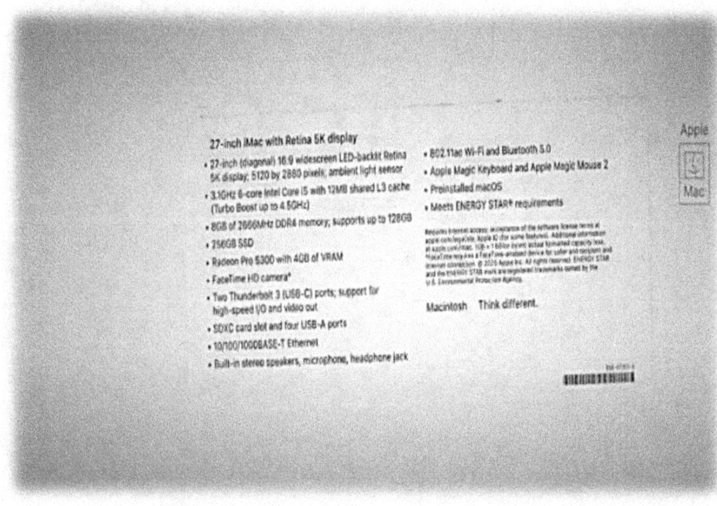

27-inch iMac with Retina 5K display

• 27-inch (diagonal) 16:9 widescreen LED-backlit Retina 5K display; 5120 by 2880 pixels; ambient light sensor
• 3.1GHz 6-core Intel Core i5 with 12MB shared L3 cache (Turbo Boost up to 4.5GHz)
• 8GB of 2666MHz DDR4 memory; supports up to 128GB
• 256GB SSD
• Radeon Pro 5300 with 4GB of VRAM
• FaceTime HD camera*
• Two Thunderbolt 3 (USB-C) ports; support for high-speed I/O and video out
• SDXC card slot and four USB-A ports
• 10/100/1000BASE-T Ethernet
• Built-in stereo speakers, microphone, headphone jack

• 802.11ac Wi-Fi and Bluetooth 5.0
• Apple Magic Keyboard and Apple Magic Mouse 2
• Preinstalled macOS
• Meets ENERGY STAR® requirements

Apple
Mac

Macintosh   Think different.

Mac

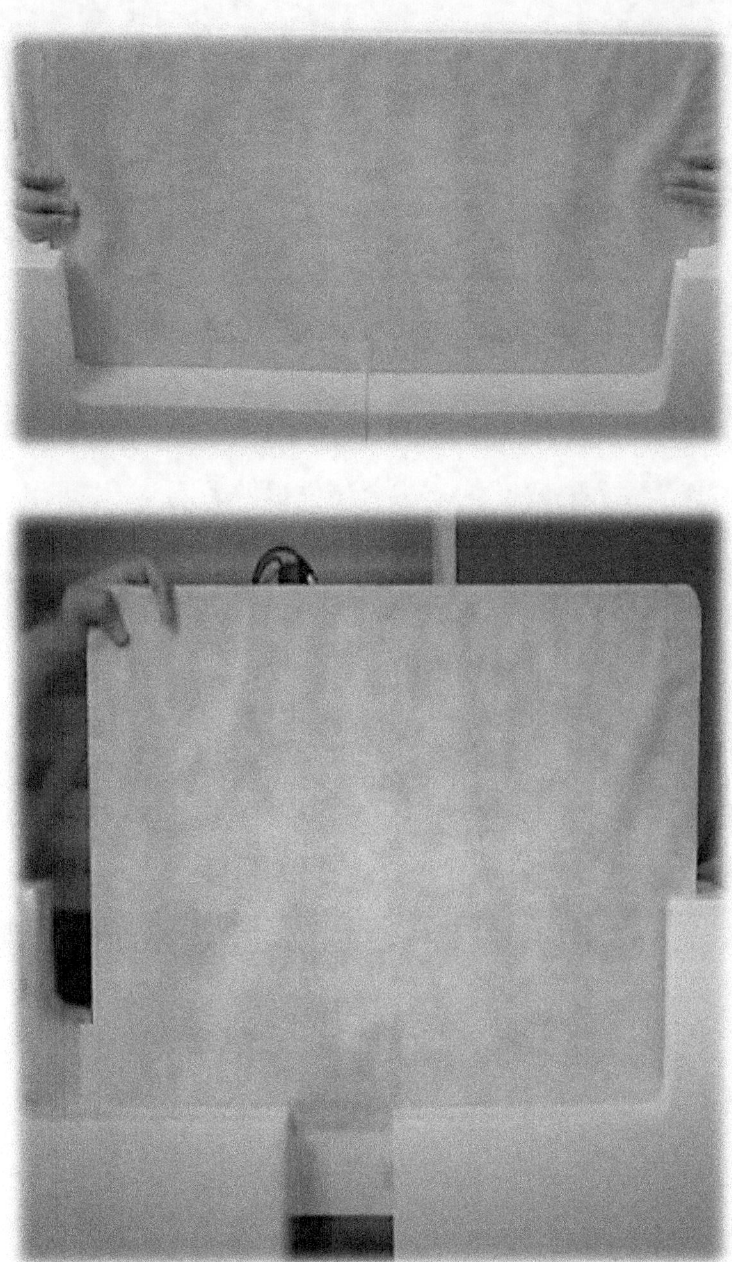

To set up how your keyboard works, click on the System Settings button; click the button at the top of the text keyboard. If your mouse needs to be recharged or reconnected, connect it to your iMac using a Lightning to USB cable.

You can also buy a Magic Trackpad 2 or Magic Keyboard separately, using a numeric keypad, and connect it to the Lightning to USB cable included with the iMac.

SET UP YOUR iMac

After switching on your iMac, the next step is to set it up using the set up wizard. When setting up your iMac, you have to select a country and region, your language and a time zone.

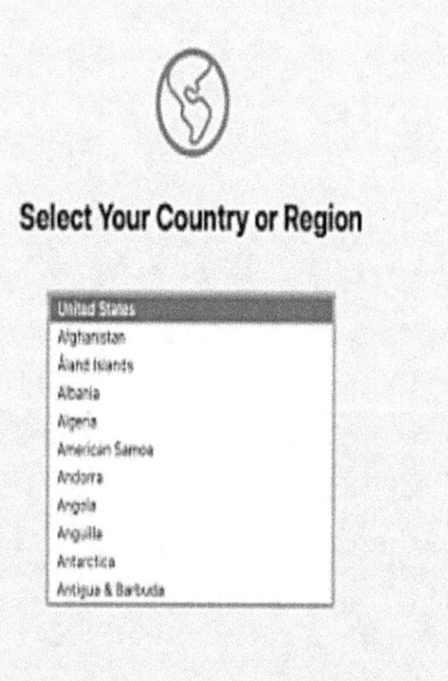

The next step is to set up your network by connecting to a Wi-Fi network.

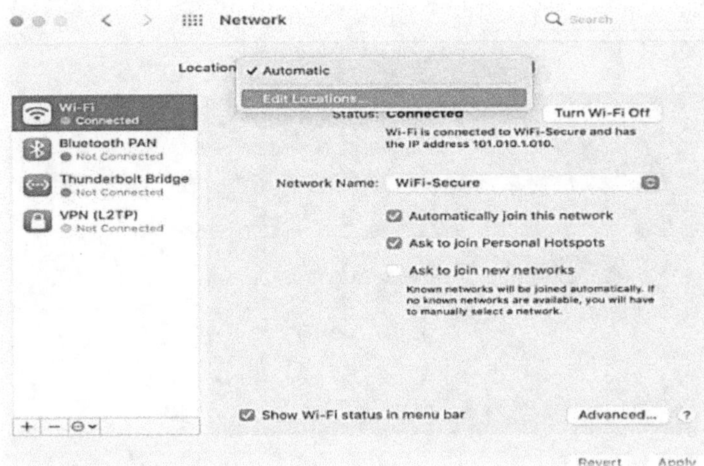

Sign in your iMac with your Apple ID which is the account you will use for everything. It gives you access to Apple services such as Apple Store, iCloud etc.

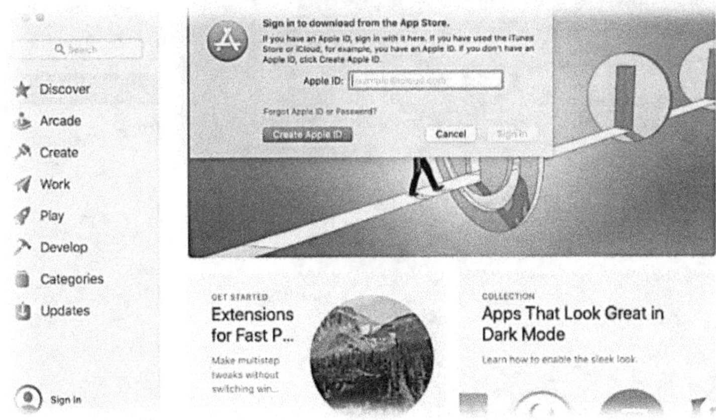

You can also activate Siri by saying the Hey Siri command on your iMac.

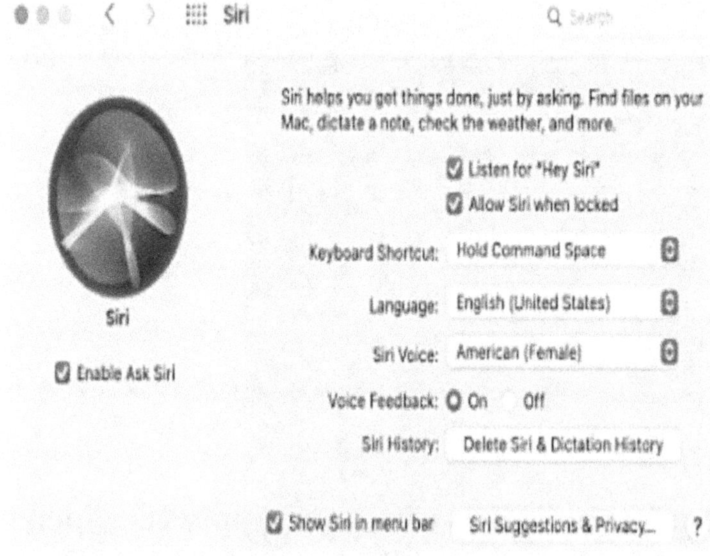

Choose the appearance: Choose Light, Dark, or Auto and adjust to the desktop look. If you want to change your selections during configuration, open System Preferences, click the General Button, and then choose the options that appear.

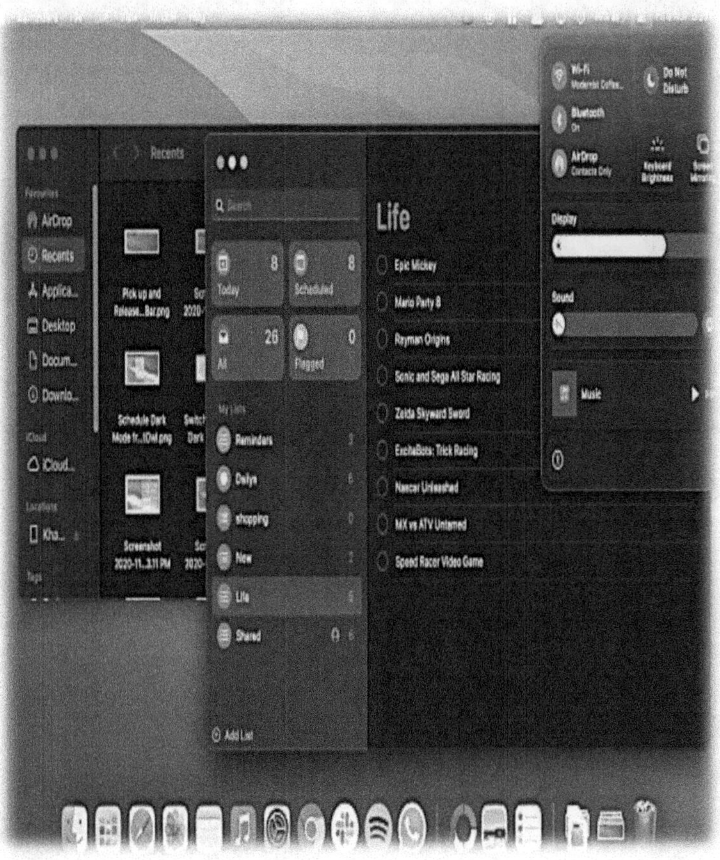

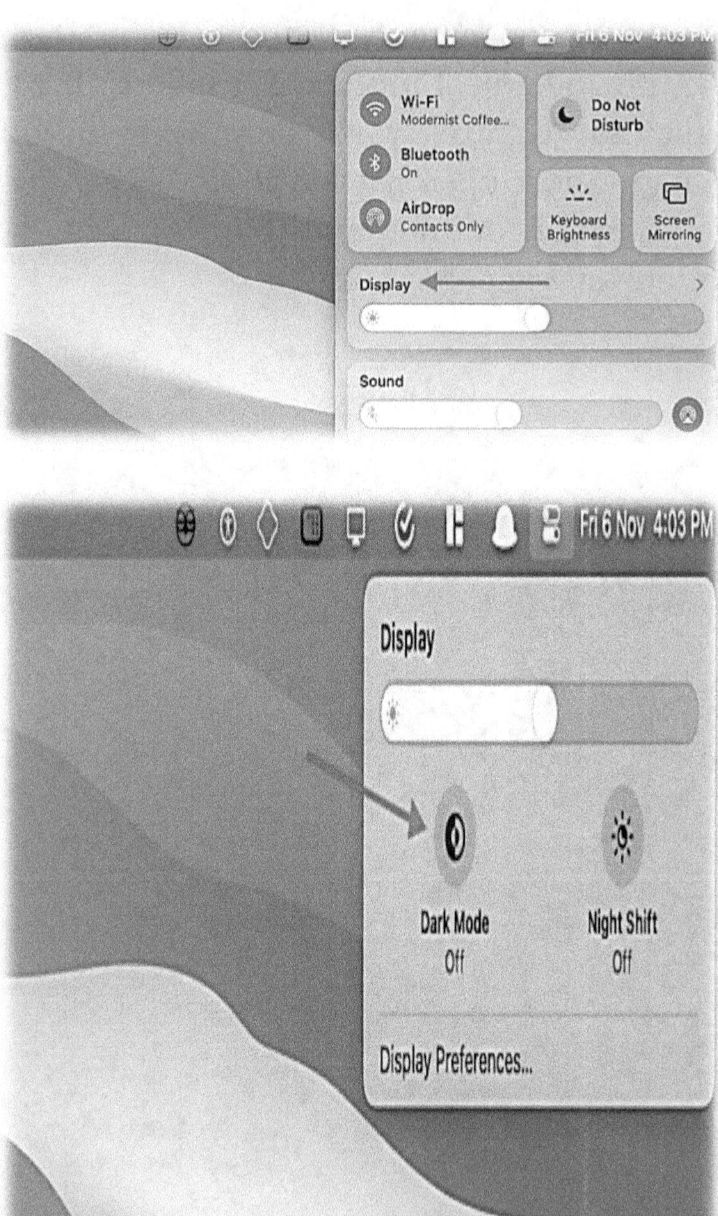

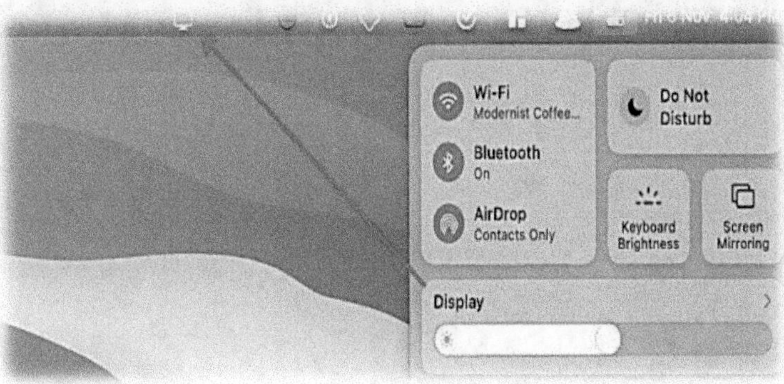

Wi-Fi
Modernist Coffee...
Bluetooth
On
AirDrop
Contacts Only
Do Not
Disturb
Keyboard
Brightness
Screen
Mirroring
Display

Use Sign in with Apple on Mac

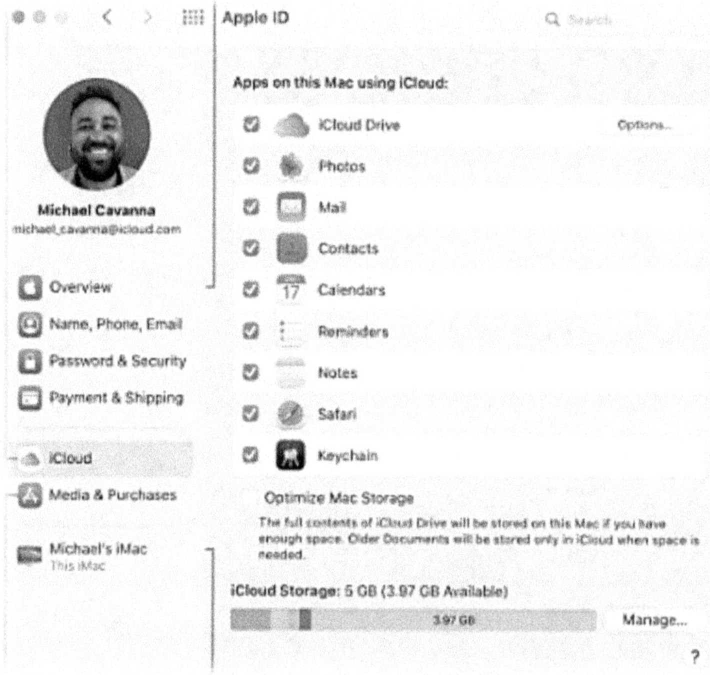

Signing in with your Apple ID allows users to easily access websites using safari and apps with the App store.

Ensure you verify your email address or fill out a simplified form each time you choose a new password and login.

If you want to open an account on an app or website on your Mac, just log in or continue using Apple if possible. Change Apple login settings for an app or website.

On a Mac, select Apple Menu> System Settings and click on Apple ID.

Click on the application or website on the sidebar to do one of the following:

Turn off email forwarding: Click the Close button.

Disable login with Apple: Click the Disable Apple ID button.

Using a Retina display

The Retina display has pixels density that the human eye cannot detect individual pixels. This feature improves your viewing experience dramatically changing the resolution of your screen

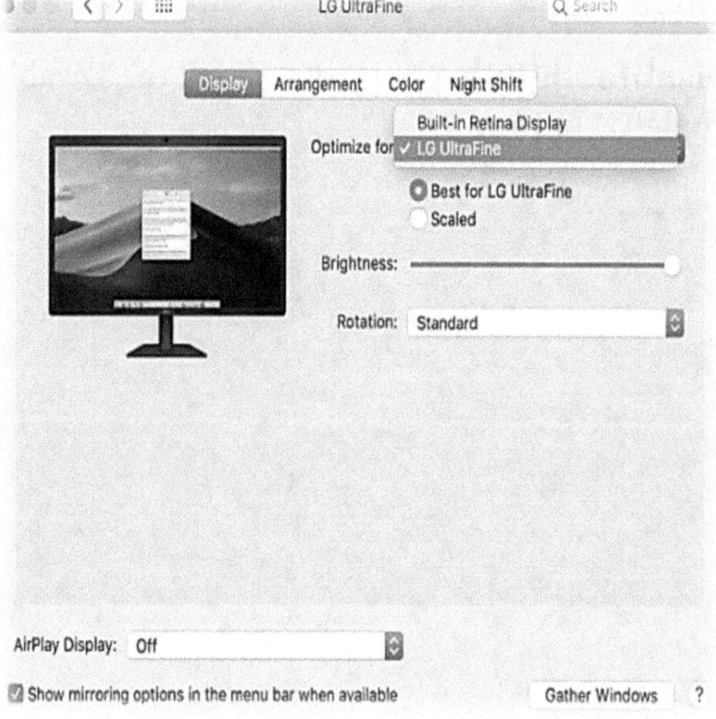

Your Mac will automatically select the default settings to suit your screen. To change the resolution:

Select the Apple menu > System Settings, and then click displays.

Windows appear less or less to free up space in the program.

If you are using an external display, and you want to expand your desktop using an external screen, you can select the desired resolution for each screen. W

To select the Scaled button, continue holding down the Option button.

If you are using an external screen to mirror the installed screen, optimize all screens selected from the menu that appears on your Mac. "Optimize" file permissions

Choose the best screen resolution for your Mac or Scaled and choose a different resolution.

When mirroring the screen, you can optimize it for your external display instead of the inbuilt display.

How to transfer data to your iMac

Transfer your data to a new iMac.

Files and settings are easy to transfer from another Mac or PC to an iMac. You can transfer data to your iMac from an old computer or a Time Machine backup on a USB storage device wirelessly or with an Ethernet cable or adapter.

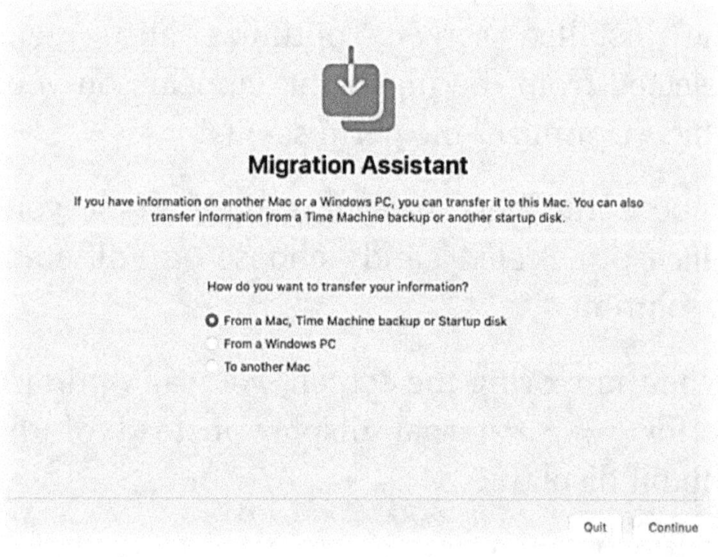

When setting up a wireless transfer on your iMac for the first time, use the configuration wizard to transfer data. If you want to move later, open the Finder window using the Migration Wizard.

Go to the application, open the Utilities application, double-click on the Migration Assistant and perform the wireless transfer. Follow the on-screen instructions.

Make sure you have both computers connected to the same network and keep computers close together during migration.

If you back up your files to another Mac storage device (such as External Disk) using

Time Machine, you can copy the file from your device to your iMac.

Copy files from storage device. Connect your device to a USB-A port, USB icon, or Thunderbolt 3 (USB-C) port on the Thunderbolt icon on the iMac, and then drag the files from there.

To set up Time Machine, ensure both your iMac and your external storage device are both connected to the same Wi-Fi network. Then open System Preferences, click on

Time Machine, and then select the option to Back up Automatically.

Back up your files using Time Machine

With Time Machine, you can save uninstalled programs, music, photos, and documents installed on your Mac.

When using a Time Machine, the Time Machine stores local snapshots that can be used to restore an earlier version of a file, even if no backup disk is attached.

Snapshots are created every hour, stored on the same disk as the original file, and stored for up to 24 hours or until disk space is required.

You have to connect your hard drive (external) to your iMac and then open the file.

Click the button to use as a backup disk on your Mac and follow the instructions.

To open the time settings, select Apple menu> System settings and then click the Time Machine button.

Desktop, menu, and help on your Mac.

After setting up your iMac, you are welcomed with the desktop which gives you the freedom to open your apps easily.

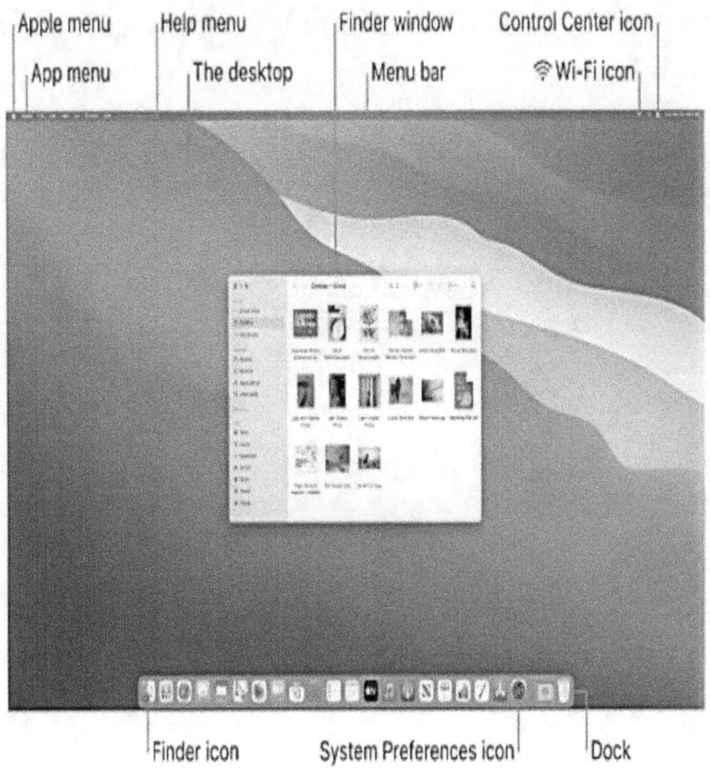

You can use the menu to select command to perform in an app.

Items on the menu depends on the apps you use. The icons located on the right part of the menu can be used to connect to a Wi-Fi network, and also to check its status.

You can also use it to open the Control Center or search using Spotlight.

The Apple menu contains commands you use frequently which are display on your screen by the left.

You can also locate the Help menu from the Menu bar.

Search with Spotlight on Mac

You can easily find documents, apps and other things on your iMac using Spotlight. You can get good recommendations from Siri suggestions on news, sports and others.

To search for something, simply click on the Spotlight icon and then press the Spotlight button or Command-Space bar.

Spotlight shows the most popular results first. Click to preview or open a popular item.

To see a preview of your search result, simply tap the Tab key and then click on the file to open it.

View results of suggested searches from Spotlight: Click on the item in front of the Spotlight icon.

View suggested search results from the web: Click on the item with the Safari icon.

Open item: Double-click it. Or select an item and click the Return button

Show file location on Mac: Select the file and press and hold the Command button, the file location will appear at the bottom of the preview.

Copy item: Drag the file to the desktop or Finder window.

You can also perform calculations using Spotlight, perform currency conversions, measurement conversions, Temperature conversions and others.

Tip: In the preview section, press the Tab key to display additional conversions.

You can delete specific folders, disks, or data types. From Spotlight Search (such as email or text).

Control center on your Mac

The Control Center integrates all your additional menus into one, giving you access to the most used controls, such as Bluetooth and AirDrop.

You can also pin your favorite things in the control center. You can change their positions using drag and drop from the Control Center to the menu, so you can easily find them with a single click to change them.

Items that open in the Control Center and Menu window. Select the controller to the left of the dock and menu opening settings, and then click the "Show in Menu Bar" or "Show in Controls" button.

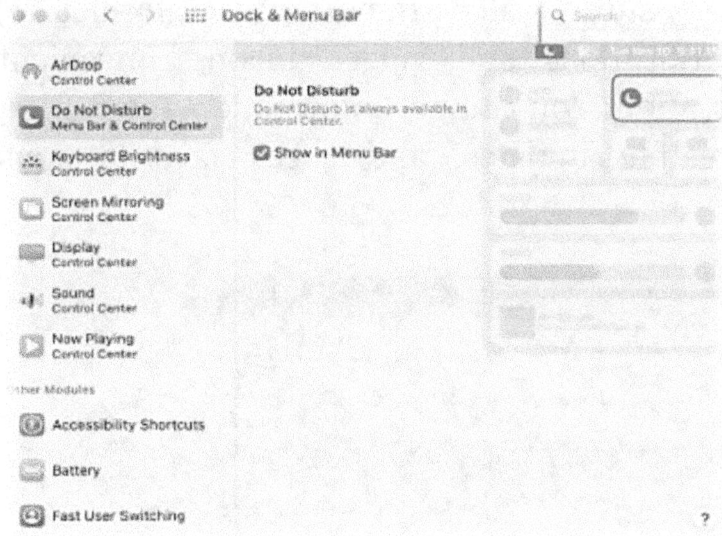

In the menu bar, you can preview where the controls will appear. Some items cannot be added or removed from the control center or menu

Tip: To quickly remove an item from the menu bar, press and hold the Command button and drag it from the menu bar.

Notification center on your Mac

The Notification Center has been redesigned to store all important information, notifications, and widgets in one convenient location. You can get information about files, weather updates, and check favorite apps here.

To open the Notification Center, simply click the date and time on your screen.

You can also give replies to emails, listen to the latest podcasts, or see more information about calendar events.

To modify your widget, click the Edit Widgets button to add, delete, or reposition widgets.

Configure notifications Open System Settings, click notifications, and select which notifications to view.

The Dock

The Dock menu is situated at the bottom of your screen, displays regularly used apps and documents.

Open an app or file, click the app icon on the Dock, or click the Launchpad icon on the Dock to see all the apps on your Mac, and then click the app you want.

Close the application by clicking the red dot in the upper left corner of the open window. However, the application is still open

Add items to the dock, drag them, and throw them where you want them.

Take the item from the dock and drag it from the dock.

Open everything on your Mac. Click the Mission Control button on your keyboard to view open windows, desktop space, full screen apps, and more.

It is easy to switch between them.

The Finder on your Mac

Use Finder to organize your files and locate them by clicking its icon on the Dock.

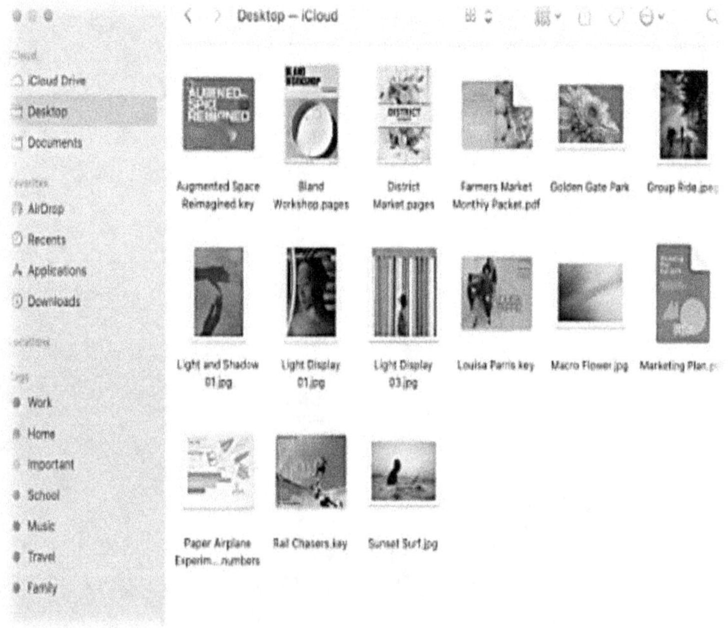

Sync Devices You can see Finder sidebar when your devices like iPhone and iPad are connected.

View Gallery- With the help of gallery view you can view selected large files as well as visually recognize images, video clips and other documents.

Desktop — iCloud
iCloud Drive
Desktop
Documents
AirDrop
Recents
Applications
Downloads
Work
Home
Important
School
Music
Travel
Family
Golden Gate Park
JPEG image - 2.9 MB
Information
Created   November 9, 2020 at 10:40
Modified   November 9, 2020 at 2:20
Last opened   Nov 10, 2020 at 9:41
Dimensions   5472×36
Resolution   240×2
Tags
Add Tags

FaceTime

With FaceTime, you can make video calls and connect with you friends using your iMac. With your iMac camera, you can call your friends. To do this, input the name/phone number/email address of the person. To make a FaceTime call with your friends and loved ones, simply click on the video button close to the name of the person you want to call.

Jane Appleseed
Audio
Video

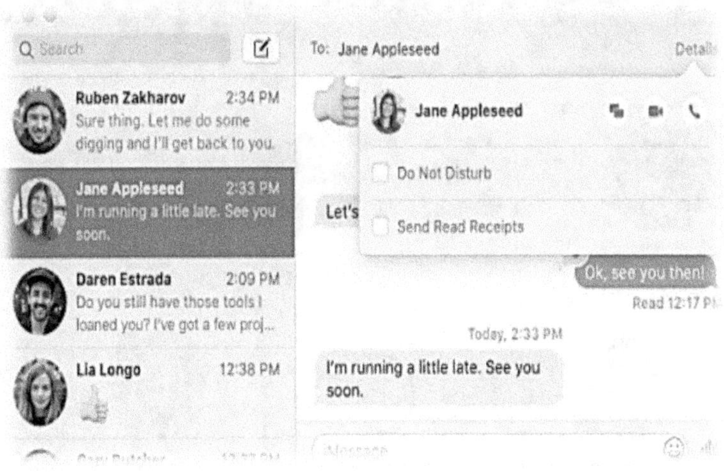
Search
Ruben Zakharov   2:34 PM
Sure thing. Let me do some digging and I'll get back to you.
Jane Appleseed   2:33 PM
I'm running a little late. See you soon.
Daren Estrada   2:09 PM
Do you still have those tools I loaned you? I've got a few proj...
Lia Longo   12:38 PM
To: Jane Appleseed   Details
Jane Appleseed
Do Not Disturb
Send Read Receipts
Let's
Ok, see you then!
Read 12:17 PM
Today, 2:33 PM
I'm running a little late. See you soon.

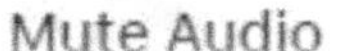

Mute Audio   End   Mute Video

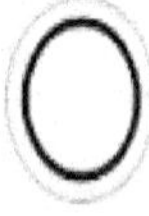

Full Screen   Camera Shutter   Sidebar

Find My

Click the People or Devices tab to find your friends or your device location.

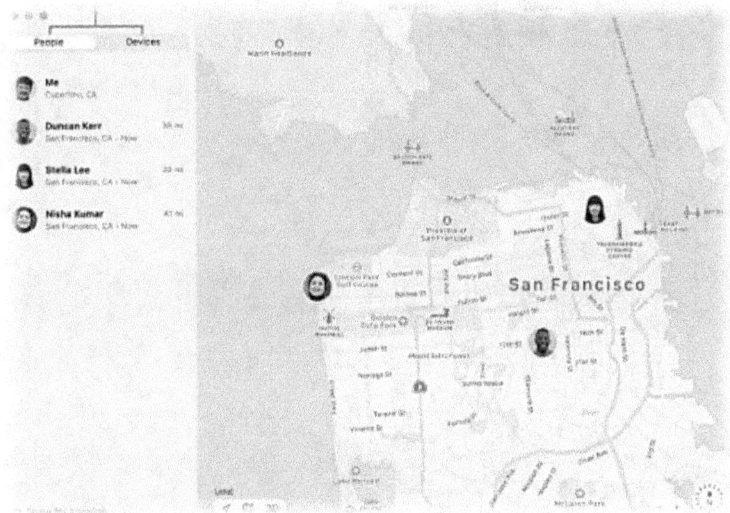

Set up location alerts automatically send notifications to your friends when you go to or from a specific location.

You can also locate a lost device using the Find My app.Simply select a device in the Devices list to pin point its location.

On the map, click on the info icon to play music to help find your device and mark it as lost so other people can't access your personal information and even remotely erase the device.

MAIL

To add an email address to use for mail, pick your account type and then enter your account information.

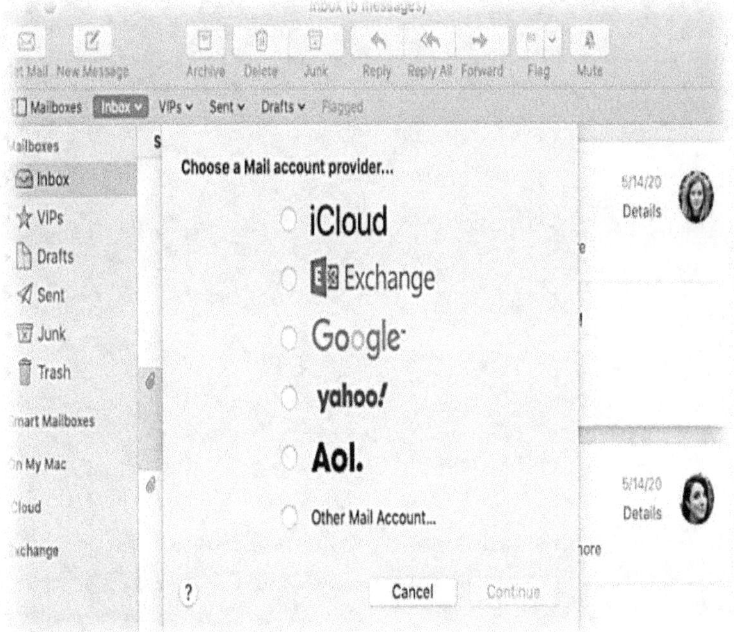

To perform this action, click on Mail and then click on Add account to select your preferred account to enter your information.

Make sure mailboxes for registration are selected.

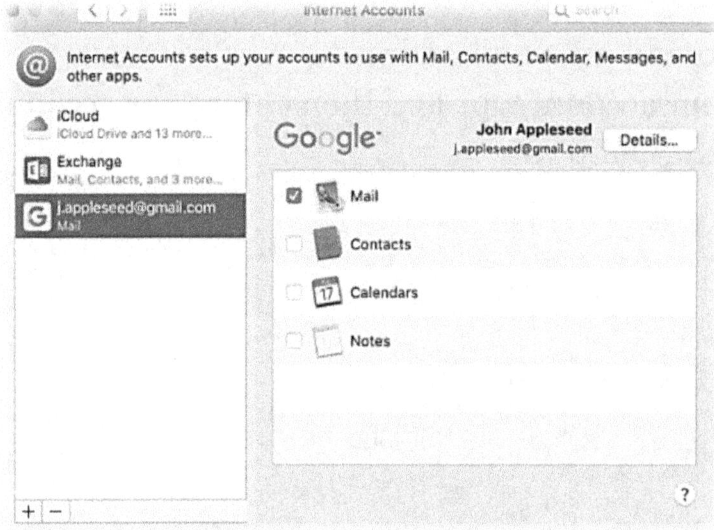

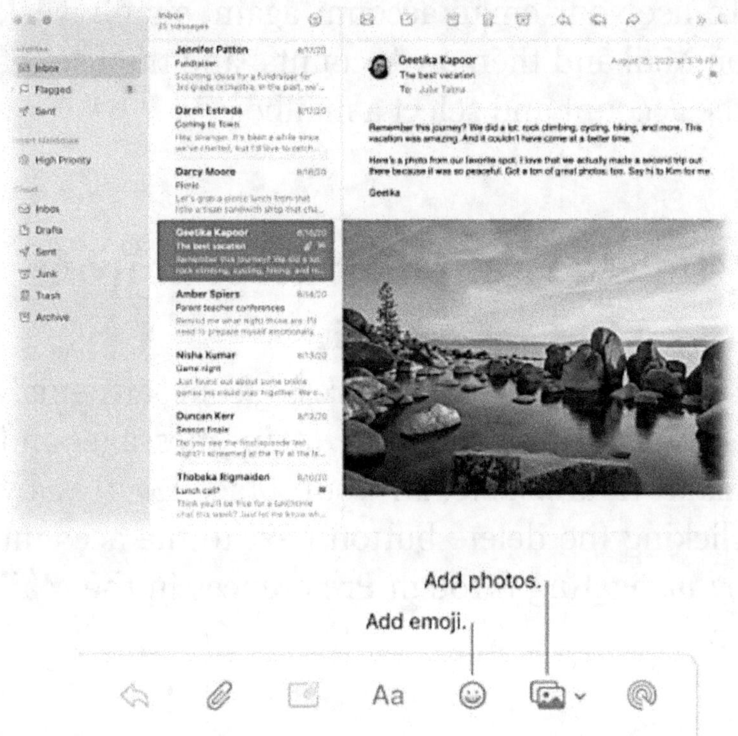

Suspend the use of email accounts.

To stop the use of an account in the Mail app on your iMac, simply click on Mail and then on Accounts.

The next move is to pick the account you want to suspend.

Pick your account and unselect the mailbox.

To use your email account again, simply click on Mail and then on Accounts, and then select the account and select a mailbox.

Delete your email account from Mail.

Deleting an email address from an email account will delete the login message and make it unusable on your Mac. Do this by clicking the delete button next to the account by navigating through Preferences in the Mail app.

Keyboard shortcuts on your Mac

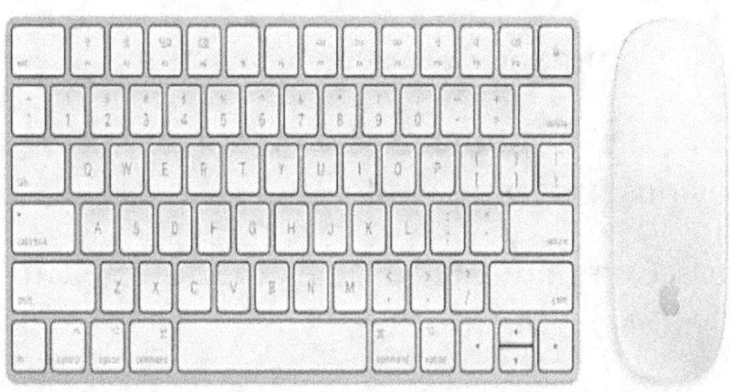

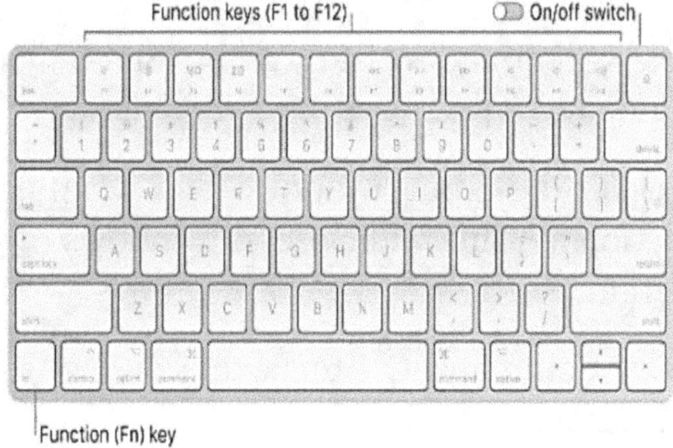

Press the Command-C key to copy the selection to memory.

Press Command-X to minimize the selection and copy it to memory.

To undo the previous command, click Command-Shift-Z Repeat.

Press Command-A to select everything.

Press the Command-M key to minimize all previous program windows.

Press Command-O to open the selected item or select the file to open.

Press the Command-P key to print the current document.

Press Command-S to save the current document.

To close the front window, click Command Selection-W This will close all windows of the program.

Press Command-Q to exit the current application.

Click the button to select the forced exit app. Command selection

Press the Command-Tab key to move from the open application to the next application you last used.

INDEX

www.ingramcontent.com/pod-product-compliance
Lightning Source LLC
Chambersburg PA
CBHW051455150726
48000CB00005B/2402